TOP CAREERS AND PROFESSIONS

Competitive Jobs / Occupations
in Modern Organizations

Calvine Odero

2022

Copyright © 2022 Calvine Odhiambo Odero

All rights reserved

The characters and events portrayed in this book are fictitious. Any similarity to real persons, living or dead, is coincidental and not intended by the author.

No part of this book may be reproduced, or stored in a retrieval system, or transmitted in any form or by any means, electronic, mechanical, photocopying, recording, or otherwise, without express written permission of the publisher.

I dedicate this work to students and professionals who have an interest in identifying competitive careers and professions in the current organizational environment.

"Luck is what happens when preparation meets opportunity."

ROMAN PHILOSOPHER SENECA

CONTENTS

Title Page
Copyright
Dedication
Epigraph
ENGINEERING — 1
INFORMATION AND COMMUNICATION TECHNOLOGY (ICT) — 2
BUSINESS AND COMMERCE — 3
SECURITY — 4
AGRICULTURE — 5
NATURAL SCIENCE — 6
MEDICINE — 7
SURGERY — 8
DENTISTRY — 9
NURSING — 10
PHARMACY — 11
EDUCATION — 12
COMMUNICATION AND PUBLIC RELATIONS — 13
HUMAN RESOURCE MANAGEMENT — 14
SOCIAL SERVICE — 15
AVIATION — 16
LAW — 17

INSURANCE AND RISK MANAGEMENT	18
PROJECT MANAGEMENT	19
RESEARCH, CREATIVITY, AND INNOVATION	20
About The Author	21

ENGINEERING

1. Electrical and Electronics Engineer
2. Civil Engineer
3. Mechanical Engineer
4. Computer Engineer
5. Telecommunications Engineer
6. Chemical Engineer
7. Industrial Engineer
8. Nuclear Engineer
9. Aeronautical Engineer
10. Architectural Engineer

INFORMATION AND COMMUNICATION TECHNOLOGY (ICT)

1. Software Developer
2. Network Administrator
3. Computer System Analyst
4. Cyber Security Specialist
5. Data Analyst
6. Information Technology Consultant
7. Computer Programmer
8. Graphic and Web Developer
9. Mobile Applications Developer
10. Database Manager

BUSINESS AND COMMERCE

1. Investment Banker
2. Actuary
3. Accountant
4. Financial Analyst
5. Marketing Manager
6. Sales Representative
7. Product Manager
8. Personal Banker
9. Company Secretary
10. Economist

SECURITY

1. Security Consultant
2. Private Investigator
3. Detective
4. Screener
5. Security Guard
6. Surveillance Officer
7. Patrol Officer
8. Security Analyst
9. Security Engineer
10. Security Officer

AGRICULTURE

1. Agronomist
2. Agricultural Engineer
3. Veterinarian
4. Agricultural Economist
5. Farm Manager
6. Soil and Plant Scientist
7. Horticulturalist
8. Grower
9. Food Technologist
10. Ecologist

NATURAL SCIENCE

1. Botanist
2. Zoologist
3. Environmental Engineer
4. Environmental Consultant
5. Park Ranger
6. Sustainability Manager
7. Aquatic Biologist
8. Nature Photographer / Videographer
9. Arborist
10. Conservation Scientist

MEDICINE

1. Psychiatrist
2. Pathologist
3. Ophthalmologist
4. General Practice Doctor
5. Clinical Radiologist
6. Anaesthetist
7. Cardiologist
8. Neurologist
9. Pediatrician
10. Dermatologist

SURGERY

1. Colorectal Surgeon
2. General Surgeon
3. Thoracic Surgeon
4. Orthopedic Surgeon
5. Pediatric Surgeon
6. Plastic Surgeon
7. Vascular Surgeon
8. Trauma Surgeon
9. Neurosurgeon
10. Critical Care Surgeon

DENTISTRY

1. General Dentist
2. Prosthodontist
3. Pediatric Dentist
4. Oral Pathologist
5. Endodontist
6. Orthodontist
7. Periodontist
8. Cosmetic Dentist
9. Family Dentist
10. Geriatric Dentist

NURSING

1. Registered Nurse (RN)
2. Cardiac Nurse
3. Certified Registered Nurse Anesthetist (CRNA)
4. Clinical Nurse Specialist (CNS)
5. Critical Care Nurse
6. Family Nurse Practitioner (FNP)
7. Emergency Room Nurse (ERN)
8. Geriatric Nurse
9. Perioperative Nurse
10. Mental Health Nurse

PHARMACY

1. Hospital Pharmacist
2. Community Pharmacist
3. Research Pharmacist
4. Home Care Pharmacist
5. Informatic Pharmacist
6. Ambulatory Care Pharmacist
7. Nuclear Pharmacist
8. Drug Safety Officer
9. Hospital Pharmacist
10. Military Pharmacist

EDUCATION

1. Special Education Teacher
2. High School Teacher
3. Elementary School Teacher
4. Kindergarten Teacher
5. Middle School Teacher
6. English as a Second Language (ESL) Teacher
7. Careers/Technical Teacher
8. Adult Continuing Education Teacher
9. Physical Education and Sports Teacher
10. Education Administrator

COMMUNICATION AND PUBLIC RELATIONS

1. Public Relations Specialist
2. Corporate Communications Officer
3. Publicist
4. Spokesperson
5. Public Affairs Specialist
6. Media Relations Coordinator
7. Marketing Communications Strategist
8. Copywriter
9. Digital Strategist
10. Journalist

HUMAN RESOURCE MANAGEMENT

1. Staffing Coordinator
2. Human Resource Associate
3. Human Resource Supervisor
4. Benefits Administrator
5. Recruiter
6. Employee Relations Manager
7. Health and Safety Officer
8. Payroll Administrator
9. Human Resource Information System (HRIS) Analyst
10. Human Resource Business Partner

SOCIAL SERVICE

1. Therapist / Counselor
2. Social Worker
3. Child Welfare Worker
4. Mental Health and Substance Abuse Social Worker
5. Behavior Analyst
6. Healthcare Social Worker
7. School Social Worker
8. Probation Officer
9. Community Outreach Worker
10. Psychologist

AVIATION

1. Pilot
2. Co-pilot
3. Air Traffic Controller
4. Airport Manager
5. Airfield Operations Specialist
6. Flight / Cabin Attendant
7. Reservation Agent
8. Baggage Handler
9. Aircraft Fueler
10. Flight Instructor

LAW

1. Constitutional Lawyer
2. Corporate Lawyer
3. Tax Lawyer
4. Advertising Lawyer
5. Employment and Labor Lawyer
6. Immigration Lawyer
7. Bankruptcy Lawyer
8. Criminal Defense Lawyer
9. Family Lawyer
10. Intellectual Property Lawyer

INSURANCE AND RISK MANAGEMENT

1. Claims Adjuster
2. Risk Analyst
3. Underwriter
4. Agent
5. Broker
6. Loss Prevention Officer
7. Investment Specialist
8. Auto Appraiser
9. Insurance Actuary
10. Insurance Investigator

PROJECT MANAGEMENT

1. Meetings, Conventions, and Events Planner
2. Monitoring and Evaluation Expert
3. Program Coordinator
4. Project Manager
5. Project Team Lead
6. Project Planner
7. Project Scheduler
8. Project Risk Manager
9. Change and Innovation Specialist
10. Project Consultant

RESEARCH, CREATIVITY, AND INNOVATION

1. Innovation Consultant
2. Change Agent
3. Business Development Manager
4. Research Scientist
5. Data Analyst
6. Creative Director
7. Business Model Designer
8. Brand Strategy Director
9. Special Projects Lead
10. Director of Strategy

ABOUT THE AUTHOR

Calvine Odhiambo Odero

A Human Resource Management (HRM) professional, currently working as a Senior Human Resource Management Officer.

www.ingramcontent.com/pod-product-compliance
Lightning Source LLC
Chambersburg PA
CBHW050328220526
45465CB00005B/2186